COLLECTIONS

A Harcourt Reading Program

New Adventures

Harcourt

Orlando   Boston   Dallas   Chicago   San Diego

Visit *The Learning Site!*

www.harcourtschool.com

CONTENTS

A Story for Pam

by Sharon Fear

illustrated by Stephen Kellogg

"Look at this ad," Teacher Dan said to the class. "It is an ad for a story."

The ad said, "Are you creative? Then write a creative story! See it in *Matt's Story Stack.*"

"This ad will be homework, Class," said Teacher Dan. "I expect you to write a story. I will send it to *Matt's Story Stack.*"

"How can I write a story?" Pam asked Teacher Dan. "What will I write?"

"What do you like, Pam? Do you like pets? You could write a pet story," suggested Teacher Dan.

"I had a pet crab," said Pam. "But it was sad to be a pet. Now my crab is in the sand. I can not write a pet story."

"Do you like flags, Pam? You could write a flag story," suggested Teacher Dan.

"I like flags," said Pam. "I have two flags. One flag is tan. It has a hat. One flag is black. It has a cat. But I have not researched flags. I can not write a flag story."

"Do you like to dance, Pam? You could write a dance story," suggested Teacher Dan.

"I like to dance," said Pam. "My dad is in the dance business. I can tap dance. I am not in the dance business. I can not write a dance story."

"You can write a story, Pam," said Teacher Dan. "You like pets. You like flags. You like to dance. You are a responsible cat. You can write a story for Matt the Cat."

Pam was sad. She sat and sat. "I can not write a story," she said. "I like pets. I like flags. I like to dance. But I can not write a creative story."

Then Pam sat up. Now she was glad. "I CAN write a story!" Pam said. "I like pets. I like flags. I like to dance. I am responsible. I will write a creative Pam story for homework! My Pam story will be in *Matt's Story Stack!* That is all there is to that!"

Think About It

1. How does Teacher Dan help Pam with her story?

2. Why do you think Pam will write a Pam story?

3. What will Pam write in her story? Think about what Pam likes. Then write the story.

Prefixes and Suffixes

Pam writes **nonstop**. *Nonstop* has two parts: *non* and *stop*. A **prefix** is a word part that is added to the beginning of a word. A **suffix** is a word part that is added to the end of a word. Prefixes and suffixes can change the meanings of base words.

Prefixes	Suffixes
dis- ("not") non- ("not") over- ("over")	-able ("able to be") -tion ("the act of") -ion ("the act of")

Knowing about word parts can help you read new words. Find a word with a prefix or a suffix in each sentence. What does the new word mean?

When I run, I run nonstop.

My story has a likable cat in it.

Add the prefix or suffix to the base word. Write a sentence with the new word.

over- look	act -ion	stack -able

NOW YOU SEE IT, NOW YOU DON'T

by Susan McCloskey
illustrated by Linda Helton

"What are you doing, Kim?" said Bill.

"I am sorting my magnets," said Kim. "I collect magnets. Look at this magnet. It is decorated to look like a squid. This one looks like a wig. Do you like the one that looks like a cat? This is my favorite. It looks like a big, pet pig."

Bill said, "Look at Miss Bliss. She is sniffing the magnet that looks like a cat. That's her favorite. Miss Bliss likes cats. You collect magnets. She collects cats. Now she has six."

Kim said, "I like magnets. See what this big one can do? It attracts the key to my building. The key gets stuck to the magnet."

Bill said, "Will the key to my building stick?" It did.

"I have to pick up my magnets now, Bill," said Kim. "I have homework to do." Then she said, "Bill! I can not find my cat magnet. I have my squid magnet. I have my wig magnet. I have my favorite pig magnet. But I do not have my cat magnet!"

?

"I will look in this drink can," said Bill.

"I will pick up the mat and look there,"
said Kim.

They didn't find the cat magnet.

Kim said, "I will lift the lid. You look in the
can. Ignore all the junk. Is the magnet there?"

Bill said, "No, it is not."

Miss Bliss said, "Yip!"

"What is it, Miss Bliss?" said Bill.

"Did you find the cat magnet?"

Then he said, "Be still, Miss Bliss! Kim, look at Miss Bliss. Do you see what I see?"

?

Kim said, "I see my cat magnet. It's
stuck to Miss Bliss!" Then she said, grinning,
"She can have my cat magnet. I am glad
she is not collecting pigs!"

Think About It

1. Where is Kim's missing cat magnet?

2. Why is Kim glad that Miss Bliss is not collecting pigs?

3. What if another magnet were missing? Kim could make an ad for the missing magnet. Write an ad for Kim. Draw a picture for the ad, too.

My Week at Camp Wonder

by Deborah Eaton
illustrated by Howard Weliver

Mom,

I like everyone at summer camp a lot.
Look what I got! It likes to get in my suitcase.
It is <u>not</u> poisonous. Doc Ross said so when it
bit Counselor Bob.

Todd

Mom,

My sock can hop! Look at this! It could win medals for hopping. What makes it hop? Something is in the sock. It is a frog! A friend got the frog in there. Now there is a big spot on it. Will you get the spots out?

Todd

Mom,

    I did something to my suitcase. It had all my rocks in it. Now it has a rip in it. Do not get mad!
I can fix it. See?

                    Todd

Mom,

   I lost my harmonica in the pond. I practiced as I sat on a big rock. Then Counselor Bob said, "STOP!" And DROP! I lost it. Everyone cheered. They like my songs a lot.

                              Todd, the Summer
                              Camp Kid

Mom,

I have something in my cabin. It's a dog! He got on my cot. Then everyone ran. It was odd! He looks like a hotdog. He's my friend. Mom, may I have him? He can sit in my suitcase. Ask Pop!

Todd

Todd,

    You have to come back now. This box is for the hotdog dog. Get him in it for the trip back. We miss you, summer camp kid!

                Mom

Think About It

1. Does Todd have fun at camp? How can you tell?

2. Why does everyone run out of Todd's cabin when the hotdog dog gets onto his cot?

3. Write a letter from Todd to Counselor Bob. Tell what happened when he got home with his new pet.

Predict Outcomes

When you read this story, did you wonder what was going to happen to Todd next? You can **make predictions**. You can think about the story facts and what you know from life. You can put those things together to make a prediction.

This web shows how you can predict what will happen in "My Week at Camp Wonder."

Fact in the Story
Todd asks his mom if he can have a pet.

What I Know
Moms want kids to be happy.

Prediction
Todd will get to take the pet home.

Making predictions can help you be a better reader. Reread page 27. Then use a web to help you make a prediction. What will happen when Todd and his new pet get off the bus?

Just a Little Practice

by Ben Farrell
illustrated by Jennifer Beck Harris

Ted went to the playground. He had his red
basketball. When he got there, he noticed Pat.
She had her basketball, too. She was getting set.

Ted pretended not to look. Then Pat's basketball
went up. It fell into the net. Ted looked at his
basketball. "Now you go in," he said to it.

As Ted aimed, Pat noticed him. He looked familiar to her. "Who is he?" she said.

Ted's basketball went up and missed. Ted ran for his ball. He noticed that Pat was looking at him. Was she looking when he missed? Did she laugh when his ball missed the net?

Pat did not laugh. She could see that he was Ted Wick. His dad, Jack Wick, was a professional. He was one of the best in the NBA. Jack Wick was Pat's favorite.

"Ted," she yelled at him, "I'm Pat. Let's test that basketball!"

Ted passed his red ball to Pat. "It was a gift," he said.

Pat passed her basketball to him. Then she aimed the red ball. It went up and in! Ted applauded.

"Now you drop one in," Pat said.

Ted aimed Pat's basketball. The ball went up. It hit the back and fell out.

"I can not get one in," Ted said.

Pat had to laugh. "Two misses are not a lot," she said.

"Do not laugh," Ted said. "My dad is coming to the playground. He has to see me make a basket. I can tell that I will not make one."

"You will," Pat said. "I'll be the teacher. It will be my job to help you make one. You are going to get the ball in the basket."

Ted missed and missed.

Then Ted got one in. Pat applauded. "See that!" she said. "You did it!"

Then Ted asked, "So, can we be friends?"

"We are friends," said Pat.

"Like best friends," big Jack Wick said.

"Dad!" Ted said. "I did not see you come to the playground!"

"I noticed what was happening," Ted's dad said. "I let the teacher do her job."

Pat looked sad. "His teacher can't dribble," she said.

"Then let's make a trade," Ted's dad said. "Now I'll be the teacher."

Pat looked up at big Jack Wick and laughed. She said, "That's the best trade yet!"

Think About It

1. How does Ted find out how to get the ball into the basket?

2. Why does Jack Wick let Pat teach Ted?

3. Think about the ending of "Just a Little Practice." What do you think happened next? Write the next part of the story. Draw a picture to go with it.

A Real Winner

by **María Cordoba**
illustrated by **Michael Carx**

It is the summer of 1988. The Olympic Games are on. On the USA swim team, Janet Evans is 17. She is not big, but she has talent. She swims like a fish! Can she help the team win the championships?

When Janet was one, she went to a swimming pool with her mom. She liked the pool! Some kids got into it to swim. Mrs. Evans asked the swimming teacher if Janet could swim in the pool.

Little Janet got her wish. She liked that pool a lot! She did not sink. She swam!

Janet kept on swimming. The pool was her playground. At 4, Janet went into swimming events. At 10, she was winning speed championships.

When Janet was 15, she went to a big swimming championship. Janet was not big, but she was strong. She was in the best of health. Some swimmers laughed at her. Not one of her teammates complained.

41

The swimmers did not laugh for long. They could see that Janet Evans had talent. They respected her skill and speed. At the end of the championships, Janet had two wins. She had shot past the fastest swimmers. Her best speed was in the 400-meter and 800-meter events.

Now Janet is at the Olympic Games! It's the 400-meter event, one of Janet's favorites. Splash! The swimmers are in the pool and swimming. Janet is fast, but she is not winning. On the last lap, she swims furiously. She flashes past the top swimmer. Janet Evans wins for the USA!

Janet wins the second 400-meter event. Then she wins the 800-meter event! In the next two Olympic Games, no one will swim the 800 meters as fast. Janet Evans is one of the best swimmers the USA has had.

Think About It

1. What things in Janet's life led her to become a champion swimmer?

2. Why do you think the author wrote Janet's story? What message did she want to give readers?

3. Do you know someone who worked hard to get to a goal? Write a short biography of that person, telling about how he or she got there.

Justin and Jessica

written by
Susan McCloskey

illustrated by
Mark Bixby

Justin looked at his desk.

"Letters, letters, letters!" he said.
"Hundreds to collect and send out. One for
the police department. One for the dance
teacher. One for the students in Miss Drum's
class. Who will get the letters there?"

"Not Ron Summs. He had an accident. He dropped a cup. He cut his hand. Not Pat Plums. She fell in the tub. She bumped her leg. That makes two accidents. Not Gil Grumps. He tripped on a rug."

Justin's expression was sad. "Who will help?" he asked.

Just then, who did he see? Jessica!
She was looking for a job.

Justin said, "You are just the one I'm
looking for. I have hundreds of letters to
get out. Can you do it, Jessica?" Jessica
jumped up and down. Yes, she could!

"Go for it, Jessica!" said Justin. "This is a rush job. I wish you luck."

Jessica obeys commands, so she went fast.

Everyone looked at her. They laughed and grinned. It was fun for Jessica.

Jessica did a winning job. The letter to the police department got there. The letter to the dance teacher got there. Best of all, the letter to the students in Miss Drum's class got there.

A bunch of the kids jumped up to see Jessica. One kid hugged her! They begged her to come back and visit.

Jessica did visit. Justin went with her. The audience clapped and clapped.

"Speech, speech!" they said.

Speech? Not from Jessica.

But Justin said it all for her—with a big grin.

Think About It

1. How do the letters get sent out?

2. Why does Jessica not make a speech?

3. Suppose the TV news wants a story about Jessica. Write the TV news story.

Story Elements

Justin and Jessica live in a small town. They have to get lots of letters out on time. These are the most important parts of this story.

Every story has three parts, or elements. The **setting** is the time and place in which the story happens. The **characters** are the people and animals in the story. The **plot** is what happens in the story.

The story map below tells about "Justin and Jessica."

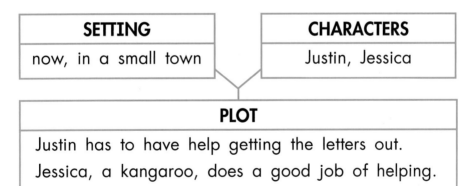

SETTING	CHARACTERS
now, in a small town	Justin, Jessica

PLOT
Justin has to have help getting the letters out. Jessica, a kangaroo, does a good job of helping.

Plan a story of your own. On a sheet of paper, make a story map like the one above to show your plan.

RACE SEA

Story by Kaye Gager

Illustrations by Donna Delich

The beach has a secret. Mom said so. I look and look for the secret. I look in a wet log. I get up on a big rock. I am eager to see the secret. What can it be?

I wish I could dig for it. Mom said no digging at all. That could be bad.

Mom said we can collect litter. I find weird junk, but I do not find the secret. I run down to the big rock. The red sun sets over the sea. We will have to look tomorrow.

The sun is setting when I run down to the beach. Mom runs with me. When we get there, there are fishing ships dancing on the sea. But what is the secret?

Mom gets up on the big rock. I get up with her. We are eager, but we have to sit patiently.

Then I see something. I see something
digging! Then I see digging all over the beach.

There they are! Is this the secret? My mom
nods. They look weird. Sand is all over them.
What are they going to do?

Then they run. Look at that speed! They run for the sea. It looks as if they have trained for it. Are they going to make it?

No! Look up there! A sea gull is going to get one of them! It misses. Mom and I clap and clap.

"Come on!" I yell to them. "You have to get to the sea!" They run down the beach to the rocks. The sea gives them a bath. The sand comes off them as they swim. Then the little swimmers go out to sea.

They are like friends now! I will be sad not to see them at the beach tomorrow.

What are they going to do now? That is
a secret of the wise sea. I wish I could get
a message to them.

I look at the sea and wish them well.
The sea gulls can not find them now. My
little friends are dancing in the sea. They
are swimming in the sun. The sea gulls
will have to have fish!

Think About It

1. What secret does the beach have?

2. Why do you think the boy's mom does not tell him what the secret is?

3. Make a postcard from the boy in the story to a friend. Draw a picture on one side to show the secret. Write a message on the other side that tells about it.

CREATURE CLICKS

by Kana Riley

All children like to watch creatures. Some adults do this as a job. They get photos that let us see how creatures survive.

Getting the photos can be hard for them. It has to be something they like to do. Just look at some of the spots they had to go to!

Marine Creatures

This sub went far down in the sea to get this shot. It is so dark that this part of the sea looks black.

Without the sun, some marine creatures still survive. Fish and crabs like the sea bottom.

The creatures there are odd. Notice how delicate some look. This spot could kill us, yet they dart and swim there without harm.

Yard Creatures

You may not have noticed some of
the bugs in the yard and in the park.
Are you curious? Look at what is out there!

This smart bug looks
like an ant. Some friends
with feathers can not tell
the two apart. They do
not like an ant for a snack.
So they do not harm this
bug. It can survive well
in the yard.

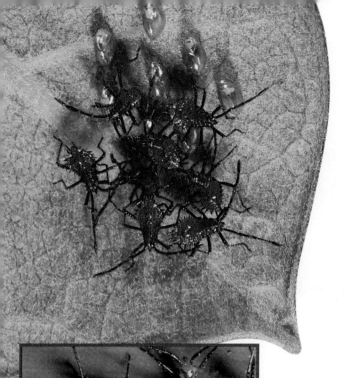

Some mom bugs park next to eggs to see them hatch. Some moms are not curious. They go off to do what they like.

This dad bug has all the eggs stuck on his back. So far he has not collapsed! It can be hard to be a bug!

Think About It

1. Where and how do the creatures in this selection live and survive?

2. How do the photos help you learn about creatures you may not have seen on your own?

3. If you could be any creature you liked, what would you choose to be? Write a paragraph explaining your choice and telling what life would be like as that creature.

Vocabulary in Context

In "Creature Clicks" you may have come to a new word you could sound out but not understand. Sometimes other words and sentences, or the **context**, can tell you what the word means.

Reread these sentences from "Creature Clicks."

This dad bug has all the eggs stuck on his back. So far he has not collapsed!

The words in the first sentence help you know that *collapsed* means "fallen down."

Now read this sentence from the first part of "Creature Clicks." What other words help you know what *marine* means?

It is so dark that this part of the sea looks black. Without the sun, some marine creatures still survive.

Help on the Trail

by Robert Newell

illustrated by Mike Harper

A chill wind whips the branches. A storm is coming. Mrs. Arnold's husband, Frank, is out hunting. Brandon, who is 12, is with him. She wishes she could telegraph them to come back.

The temperature drops. A bad snowstorm starts. The wind makes the snow hit hard, like splinters.

Are Frank and Brandon lost? They could freeze out there! Did they go north from the ranch or south? Mrs. Arnold can't tell which, but some dogs can.

How do dogs find someone who is lost? They sniff something that belongs to him or her. Then they sniff along the trail, looking for that smell.

Which dogs can do this? Smart dogs. Strong dogs. They have to like adults and children. And they have to have a teacher.

Dogs like this do not just sit and fetch. Starting as pups, they hunt for the teacher over and over.

When someone is lost, dogs like Champ and Patches start sniffing. They are hunting for his or her smell. A snowstorm can't stop them from doing the job. They will find the trail.

This dog stops and barks. It's a signal that he sees someone. ▶

◀ The drifts of snow are up to this dog's chin. She has to inch along. But just watch—she'll get there!

Patches has a red harness and a bell. The bell signals that help is coming. ▶

Help did get to Frank and Brandon Arnold. Some dogs started out at the ranch. They hunted to the north and to the south. They guided friends to the Arnolds. Frank and Brandon had gotten lost. They got chilled, but they did not freeze in the storm.

Frank said, "Thanks so much!" What did Brandon do? He had big, big hugs for the dogs!

Think About It

1. How do Frank and Brandon Arnold get back home?

2. Why would dogs be good at finding someone who is lost?

3. What do you think Brandon told his class about being lost in the snowstorm? Write Brandon's story.

The Dinosaurs' Brunch

by Deborah Eaton

Morris Thor set a trap. It was all sticks and thorns.

What was that?

A snort?

Morris yanked on the cord.

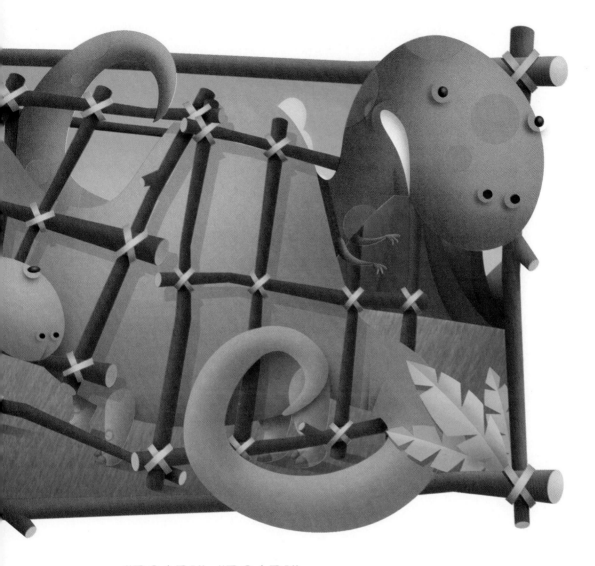

"ROAR!" "ROAR!"

Morris had trapped two dinosaurs! Two was enough. More than enough! The trap was crowded. More than crowded! One was as big as two horses. And that was the short one!

"ROAR!" One roar was like storms storming.
"ROAR!" One roar was like lava erupting.
The dinosaurs tore at the trap.
Morris's twin, Doris, ran for safety.
"Dinosaurs!" she yelled. "Run, Morris!"

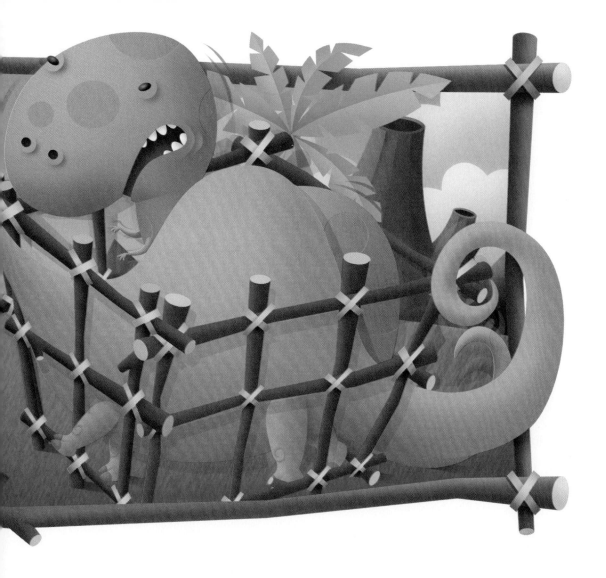

"No," said Morris. "I set the trap, and now I have two big pets."

"Morris," said Doris, "the dinosaurs you trapped are not peaceful ones. They do not like plants. What if they escape? Think what they will have for brunch. YOU on a fork!"

"ROAR!" "ROAR!"

Morris looked at the trap. The top part
was torn.

"They do look sort of mad," he said. "Well,
I have a chore to do."

Morris ran to the egg store. He looked at
all the eggs. "This is not enough," he said.
"Do you have more?"

Then Morris mixed and poured. He had
to be quick. The trap was getting worn out.

"Come and get it!" Morris said. He had
brunch for the dinosaurs—a big omelet and
two corn muffins.

"ROAR!" "ROAR!"

Gobble, gobble, gobble.

They liked it!

"Mmm!" the short dinosaur said. "MORE!"
He looked at Morris. He licked his lips.
Morris yelled, "Doris! HELP!"
Off he ran.

"What is his problem?" the short dinosaur
asked. "I was just going to ask if he could
make apple dumplings."

"He's going to get help," Stretch said. "What
do you think we will have for brunch tomorrow?"

Think About It

1. What happens after Morris sets his trap? What does he plan to do?

2. Why does Morris run off when the dinosaur licks his lips?

3. What do you think will happen tomorrow? What will the dinosaurs do? What will Morris and Doris do? Write about your ideas and draw a picture.

A NEW BEST FRIEND

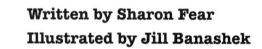

Written by Sharon Fear
Illustrated by Jill Banashek

"Write to me!" Howard shouted.

"I will!" Rick shouted back. The car and the moving van started off. They went down the block, around the playground, and beyond it.

Rick was moving to a new town.

"I wish I could go, too," Howard said to his friend Beth.

"Will you be lonely without him?" asked Beth.

"He was my BEST friend," Howard said seriously.

"Help me with my kite," said Beth. Howard held the kite. Beth unwound some string. She fastened the string to the kite.

"You can get a new best friend," said Beth. Howard frowned. "How? Who?"

Howard's dog bounded up to them. Beth picked up a stick and tossed it. "Get it, Bow Wow!" Beth shouted.

"How about Jack?" she asked.

"Jack does not like Bow Wow," Howard said.

"How about Norman?" said Beth.

"Norman who?" asked Howard.

"His dad has a brown mustache," said Beth.

"Bow Wow does not like Norman," said Howard.

Bow Wow growled.

"See," said Howard.

Howard picked up his basketball, dribbled it, and shot. It rimmed around and fell out. He passed it to Beth. She dribbled around him. She shot. Pow! She sank it!

"Wow!" shouted Howard. "Outstanding!"

"I have a secret gift," teased Beth. They played on trading shots.

"Chuck!" she said. "Chuck could be your new best friend."

Howard frowned. "Chuck can't play basketball," he said. "Not like you."

"How about Ben?" said Beth.
"Can't swim," said Howard.
"Patrick?" said Beth.
"Can't play chess," said Howard.
"Carl!" shouted Beth.
"Can't do a cartwheel," said Howard.
"I give up," said Beth, doing a cartwheel.

Then it came to him. Beth was his friend.
She was a girl, but she was the best.

"How about you?" Howard said.

She looked at him. "Can you dribble with
your left hand?" she teased again.

"Yes," said Howard.

"You wish!" She laughed out loud. "Well,
let's work on it now." She passed him the
basketball.

"Outstanding!" said Howard.

Think About It

1. Why is Howard looking for a new best friend? Who will be his best friend now?

2. Why does it take Howard so long to know who his new best friend will be?

3. Howard is going to write to Rick. What do you think he will say? Write a letter for Howard to send.

Synonyms and Antonyms

When Beth makes a good shot, Howard tells her it is *outstanding*. The author could have used another word that means the same thing.

Synonyms are words that have almost the same meaning. **Antonyms** are words that have opposite meanings.

This chart shows a synonym and an antonym for a story word from "A New Best Friend."

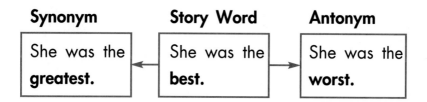

Synonym	Story Word	Antonym
She was the **greatest.**	She was the **best.**	She was the **worst.**

Authors pick words that help describe what they are writing about. Readers look for clues in the author's words to help them understand new words and ideas.

Think about something you can describe. Write a sentence. Next, rewrite the sentence using a synonym and then an antonym. How does the meaning change?

That tree is _____.

story by
Sydnie Meltzer Kleinhenz

illustrated by Joe Cepeda

STAR TIME

Mom and Dad,

Help! Camp could not be worse! I went to my first Stars class. I had my star chart. I wanted to look up at the stars. Do you know what? Stars is for campers who want to <u>be</u> stars. It's not for campers who want to <u>see</u> stars! We all have to perform in a talent show. I prefer watching to acting. I want to quit. Come get me!

Forget it. You'll get this letter after the talent show is over. I'll think of something.

I miss you,
Kirsten

94

Kirsten could see Karen and Robert recite lines from a play. Carmen and a girl from cabin 2B did handstands. Josh played the camp song on his horn. Jennifer twirled in her costume. Ernest was making up a poem about bugs.

Kirsten sat alone. She looked at her letter. She looked at the river far away. What was she going to do? She went back to her cabin to get her gym bag.

At dusk, Kirsten saw Gilbert. "I do not know what to do for the talent show," he said. "I can't act or make up a poem. I do not know any tricks." He kicked the dirt and hollered, "GROWL!"

"Wow! That was as loud as a dragon," said Kirsten.

"That is my one talent," said Gilbert frowning. "I can be loud."

Kirsten clapped. "I know what we can do!"

Kirsten got her star charts and lantern out of her gym bag. "There are billions of stars," she said. "Some make patterns of things. Look at this."

She stuck a pin into different spots on a card. She put the card over her lantern. It flashed the pattern of stars on a big rock. "Take the lantern. Now do your dragon growl."

Gilbert growled. Kirsten went to the rock and showed Gilbert the pattern in the stars. "Here's the Dragon," she said.

Gilbert and Kirsten got a long, black cloth from the camp director. They pinned it up at the front of the Stars platform. Gilbert helped Kirsten cut spots out of the cloth.

They were all grins when it was their turn at the talent show. Kirsten held her gym bag of props. Gilbert held a funnel to his mouth. They went to the back of the cloth. The campers looked puzzled.

Kirsten flashed her lantern on the back of the cloth. She said, "These are the Big Dipper and the Little Dipper." Gilbert made the sound of dripping water.

For Pegasus, Gilbert made the sound of wings flapping. For the Archer, he made the ping of the string. For the Twins, he made baby sounds. They ended the show with Gilbert's loud growl for the Dragon. The campers clapped and clapped.

Mom and Dad,

Camp is better now! I was in the talent show with my pal, Gilbert. We got to <u>be</u> stars and <u>see</u> stars. Lots of campers are enjoying making star cards for their lanterns. Now we have a new and different Stars class.

Forget about my wanting to quit. I'm having fun!

Love,
Kirsten

Think About It

1. What is Kirsten's problem? How does she fix it?

2. What gives Kirsten an idea for something to do in the talent show?

3. Make a poster for the Stars talent show. Use words and pictures to tell about the show.

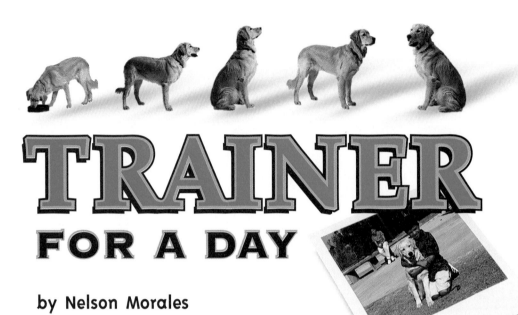

TRAINER
FOR A DAY

by Nelson Morales
photographs by Michael Campos

Here I am with our special pup, Jake. That's my sister Janet on the bench.

Jake is Janet's dog for now. Mom, Dad, and I all play with Jake and have lots of fun with him. We work hard on Jake's training, too.

Jake is going to be a working dog. He will help someone who can't see.

Jake will be a good working dog. He is very gentle. He likes everyone, and he can cheer anyone up! He is very smart, too. After his training, he will have lots of important skills for his work.

Janet and Jake are part of a special program. In this program, kids can help train a working dog. When the training is over, Janet will have to give Jake up. That will be hard for all of us. Still, we are all glad to know that Jake will be helping someone.

Jake has to be comfortable anywhere he is taken. That's why Mom and Dad take Jake to work now and then. We take him to shops and parks. He comes with me when I have an appointment with the doctor. Wherever we go, Jake can go. It's part of his training.

Jake likes to go on car trips. He likes to go on the bus, too. All these trips will help Jake know how to be a good working dog.

Dad and I like to watch the planes take off and land. Jake comes with us. He sits still and watches the planes. I wish I could know what Jake is thinking!

Mom, Dad, Janet, and I are going to take a plane trip. Jake will come with us. That trip will be one of the best parts of training Jake.

When I got to take Jake to class, Janet had to tell me what to do. "One skill Jake has to have is to be calm when someone approaches him. Be firm and confident when you tell him what to do. Do not forget to let him know when he is doing a good job."

Janet had a lot to say! At last, Jake and I were off.

When we got there, Jake and I went into the playground. Lots of kids were playing on the equipment. They jumped down and rushed over to see Jake.

To some of the kids I said, "Do not approach Jake too fast. Do not yell at him."

To some I said, "It's all right. Jake is a very gentle dog."

Jake let all the kids pet him. "Good dog, Jake," I said.

Jake's training is going well. Maybe I will be the next one to have a special pup like Jake.

Think About It

1. Why does Janet work hard to train Jake?

2. Why is going lots of places part of Jake's training?

3. If you were Jake's trainer for a day, what would you do? Make a plan for the day. Tell why you would do each thing.

Main Idea

Jake is in training to be a working dog. That is the **main idea** in "Trainer for a Day." The main idea is the message the author wants to tell. To find the main idea, ask yourself, "What is this selection mostly about?"

In the web below, the main idea is in the center circle. The other sentences tell more about the main idea. Find the main idea in the paragraph.

Jake will be a good working dog. He is very gentle. He likes everyone, and he can cheer anyone up. He is very smart, too.

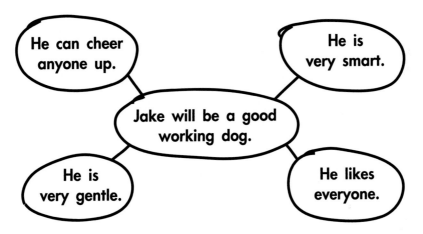

Sometimes the author states the main idea in a sentence. Sometimes readers have to figure it out on their own. Read a paragraph in a science textbook. Can you find the main idea?

written by Anthony Carmendolla
illustrated by Jeff Shelley

It was a summer camp ball game in June. The
Reds were playing the Tans. The Reds were up in the
top of the last inning. The score was Tans 3, Reds 2.
With two outs, the bases were filled with Reds.

Up to then, Jeff had been pitching well for the
Tans. Now he looked sad. Ben ran over from first
base. Tim came out from in back of home plate.

"Cheer up," Ben said. "One out wins the game."

"Yes, and one hit puts the Reds on top," Tim added.

"They may bunt," Jeff said. "They can see that I'm no ballhawk. They just may want to settle for a tie for now."

"Jeff," Ben said, "depend on Tim and me to look out for bunts. You concentrate on pitching."

"Play ball!" the ump yelled.

"All right," Ben said. "Let's see that they don't score."

Jeff looked at the Red player who was up to bat.
Was he going to bunt for a tie? Jeff could not know.
He got set and pitched.

This batter was not bunting. He let the pitch go
by for a ball. He did not swing at all.

"Let him hit!" Ben hollered. "We'll get him out!"

Jeff pitched his best pitch. The Red player's hit
was a pop-up.

"I hope Ben can catch it," Jeff said.

Ben ran back, but the pop-up fell in. The Red players were running. As Ben ran for the ball, two of them came home to score. When Ben got the ball in to Tim, the Reds were up by one run.

Ben came over to Jeff. "That missed catch was my fault," he said. "We can still make it up. One out, and we get to bat."

"I know," Jeff said. "I'll get this batter out."

The next Red player up at bat hit the ball toward Ben again. Ben dove for the ball and came up with it.

"Good catch!" Jeff shouted out.

"Now we score some runs," Ben yelled back.

The first Tan player up struck out. Then Tim came up. He let one pitch go by for a ball. Then he got a hit. After that, one more Tan player was out, and Tim stole a base. There were two outs.

"I'm up," Jeff said. "Do you want someone to bat for me? We can use a big hit."

"No," Ben said, "you can hit as well as anyone. Just get up to the plate and concentrate. Watch for the pitch you can hit. Then slam it."

Jeff did what Ben said. He let one pitch go. It wasn't the pitch for him. Then he swung at a pitch. His hit shot up over first.

One of the Reds' outfielders ran after the ball. As Jeff got to first, he watched the ball vanish over the outfielder. He couldn't catch it. It was a home run! The game was over!

Jeff trotted around the bases, and his teammates clapped. Jeff's home run was the best hit of the game.

After Jeff stepped on home plate, he went over to Ben. "You were right, Ben," he said. "You helped me get that home run."

"No," Ben said, "it was your hit."

Jeff grinned. "Yes," Jeff said, "but you are special to all of us. You help us play like a team."

"That's right," Tim added. "You are something special, Ben, and a good friend, too."

Think About It

1. Why is Ben important to the team?

2. How does Ben help Jeff make a home run?

3. Jeff keeps a diary. What do you think he writes in his diary after the game in "Coach Ben"? Write his diary entry.

ROOM to SHARE

written by Julio Mendez

illustrated by Sandy Appleoff

Mike woke up and smiled. His grandpa was coming. That was the good news. Then Mom gave Mike the bad news.

"Make your room look good," Mom said. "Make room for Grandpa Ike, too. He'll be your roommate."

Mike sat right up. This was unexpected. Mike liked his grandpa, but he liked his room, too. It was all his. It was where he went when his baby sisters acted like pests.

"Mom," Mike griped. "My room is tiny. It's just the right size for me."

Mike's mom glanced over at Mike.

"In this family, we share," she said.

Mike longed for the comfort of a room for himself, but he said, "OK, Mom. I'll do it for the family."

"Thanks, Mike," Mom said. "That's fine."

She left for work, where she filled prescriptions.

119

When his grandpa came, Mike smiled and hugged him. At the same time, he was thinking about sharing his room.

"I know I'll like being your roommate," Grandpa Ike said.

"Me, too," said Mike, but he could not look at his grandpa.

"We'll have a good time," Grandpa Ike went on. "Just the two of us."

At bedtime, Mike and his grandpa went to Mike's room. Mike's baby sisters wanted to come, too. They wanted attention from their grandpa.

"No," Grandpa Ike said, "not this time. This time it's just us men."

He winked at Mike, and Mike winked back. Grandpa Ike's good cheer was contagious. Maybe this would not be so bad after all.

In Mike's room, Grandpa Ike unpacked his suitcase. He pulled out a wide blanket and made a tent with it.

"Here we are in Camp Mike and Ike," he said.

Then he pulled out a tiny TV.

"We may be camping," he said, "but we still like the comforts of home."

Then Grandpa Ike got out a pile of snacks. He cut some pie for Mike.

"Now I'll tell you a family story," he said. "I'll tell you what your mom was like when she was nine. She was quite a bit like your baby sisters."

Mike had fun. He and his grandpa giggled and laughed. The time went by fast. Mike got very tired. He got into the top bunk to lie down.

Grandpa Ike said, "I like this, but it's too bad you have to share your room."

Mike smiled a wide smile.

"That's all right," he said. "There's room enough to share, and you are a fine roommate."

Think About It

1. How does Grandpa Ike make having a roommate fun for Mike?

2. Why can't Mike look at Grandpa when he says "Me, too"?

3. After Grandpa Ike goes home, he will write Mike a thank-you note. Write the note he might send.

Many Moons Ago

by Diane Hoyt-Goldsmith
illustrated by Franklin Ayers

Many moons ago, in the far north, it was dark all the time. This was because the sun, the moon, and the stars were hidden in three bags. The bags hung inside a mean man's house.

At that time, animals were very clever. They could sing and tell stories. Some could play tricks on those who were around.

Raven was one skillful creature. He could go as swiftly as an arrow over the land. Gazing down, he could see things happen from miles away.

Like all the rest of the animals, Raven was tired of the dark. He had a plan.

The mean man had a wife but no children. One time the wife was outside. Something made a tiny sound. "Gah! Gah!" it cried. She looked around and found a baby, all alone. She did not know the baby was Raven.

"Look," she said to the man. "I have found a baby who needs us." Then she made a big feast. She wanted to feed the baby. "Eat this," she said. "It's good for you."

Raven would not eat. All he would do was say "Gah! Gah! Gah!" He got louder and louder and louder.

The wife was sad. "What can we do?" she asked the man. "Our little baby will not eat."

"Maybe he wants a plaything," said the man. He looked at the three bags. He got down the bag with the stars and gave it to Raven. Raven stopped making his sounds and smiled.

Then Raven opened the bag. The stars tumbled out, and up they went. They arranged themselves into twinkling pictures of animals.

129

Raven smiled a little. Then he started to make his sounds again. "Gah! Gah! Gah!"

"Give him more things," said the wife. The man gave Raven the bag with the moon. When Raven opened the top, out came the moon. It rose over the canyon and lit up the dark. "Gah!" said Raven.

"No more playthings for you!" the man said.

When they were all in bed, Raven made more loud sounds. The wife was sad. The man tossed and turned. He could not sleep. "Gah! Gah! Gah!" Raven cried.

The man got down the last bag. He gave it to Raven. When Raven opened the bag, out came the sun, red and hot.

Up, up, up rose the sun. It lit up the deepest canyons and the darkest forests. All the animals could feel its heat.

Clever Raven shed his costume and showed what he was. "Gah!" he shouted with pride.

He still has not stopped. Even now you can hear him calling, "Gah! Gah! Gah!"

Think About It

1. How does Raven make the world different?

2. Why do you think Raven will not eat any of the feast the wife made?

3. How does the world look before Raven lets out the stars, the moon, and the sun? How does it look afterward? Draw two pictures. Write sentences to go with your pictures.

Sequence

Raven gets the stars, the moon, and the sun from the mean man. This story tells about these events in time order, or sequence. Often writers use time-order words to show the order in which things happen.

first	next	then	later	finally

This chart shows the order of some events from "Many Moons Ago."

First, the woman finds the baby and brings him home.

↓

Next, she cooks a big feast, but the baby won't eat.

↓

Then the baby cries and cries.

↓

The man gives the baby his bag with the stars.

Think about the other events in "Many Moons Ago." What happens next? What is the last thing that happens in the story?

Plan your own story about something Raven does. Think about the events in your story. Draw a chart like the one above to show those events in time order.

Grandpa Tells Why

by Ann W. Phillips
illustrated by C.D. Hullinger

One year, the rains did not come to the plains. Day after day, the sun's rays burned down. The air was hot, and the ground was hard.

There was no hay. There was no grain. Many animals traveled very far away to look for things to eat.

The animals that stayed grumbled with hunger.

"We must have a council meeting," they said.

So a summons went out. Animals came from all over.

At the meeting, Gray Rabbit, Long-Tail Snake, and Grandpa Turtle were the wisest and bravest. They were the leaders.

"We can't stay here," the animals said. "We must find enough to eat."

So the animals set off over the plains staying close to their leaders.

They passed by many dangers during their hunt for a meal. Always Gray Rabbit, Long-Tail Snake, or Grandpa Turtle kept them safe.

At last they found a tree with good things to eat on it. The problem was the good things were way up on the branches. The animals could not reach them. They became alarmed.

"I know about this tree," said Grandpa Turtle. "We must say its name."

"Tell us why," the animals cried.

"It is a secret of the plains. The tree will let us eat when we repeat its name three times," said Grandpa Turtle.

"How can we find out the tree's name?" asked Gray Rabbit.

"The king knows it," said Grandpa Turtle. "It is his duty to tell it to us."

Gray Rabbit volunteered to go see the king.

The king had a fine mane of hair and a long tail. He looked angry to see Gray Rabbit.

Gray Rabbit was terrified, but she asked, "What is the tree's name?"

"Please-May-We," said the king. "Now go away."

On the way back Gray Rabbit fell in a hole. When she got out, she'd forgotten the tree's name.

"I will go this time," said Long-Tail Snake.

Long-Tail Snake traveled across the plains to see the king.

The king was very angry to be bothered again.

"What nonsense is this?" he growled.

Long-Tail Snake was terrified, but he asked, "What is the tree's name?"

"I will say it one more time," said the king. "The tree's name is Please-May-We. Now go away."

On the way back Long-Tail Snake fell in a hole. He was so shaken by the fall that he forgot the tree's name.

Now all the animals were afraid.
Who could get the name for them?

"I will go," said Grandpa Turtle. He started off
over the plains.

The rest of the animals stayed by the tree
and waited.

At last Turtle came to the king.

The king was very, very angry.

But Grandpa Turtle was not alarmed.

"What mischief is this?" roared the king.
"I told Gray Rabbit and Long-Tail Snake the name.
I will not tell YOU that the tree's name is Please-
May-We."

"All right," said Grandpa Turtle.
He started back over the plains.
The animals waited and waited.

They were terrified that Grandpa Turtle would not make it back.

It took Grandpa Turtle many days, but he did not forget. Even when he fell in the hole he did not forget.

All the way across the plains he said the tree's name.

At last he came to the tree.

"What is the tree's name?" the animals asked.

"Please-May-We," said Grandpa Turtle.

The animals repeated the name three times, then the tree bent down.

It laid good things to eat on the ground.

The animals ate and ate until they were satisfied.

From then on, Grandpa Turtle was the first one the animals asked when they wondered why something was the way it was.

Think About It

1. Why can't Gray Rabbit and Long-Tail Snake get things to eat from the tree? How does Grandpa Turtle get the tree to help the animals?

2. Why do you think Gray Rabbit and Long-Tail Snake are terrified of the king?

3. Rabbit, Snake, and Turtle each try to solve the problem of the tree. Make a chart to show how these characters are alike, and how they are different.

This Is My Story

by Diane Hoyt-Goldsmith
photographs by Lawrence Migdale

When I was a girl, I loved to read. If my mother needed me, she could find me sprawled on my bed reading. My favorite stories were about faraway lands or other times.

I loved art, too. I drew and painted and cut and glued. I worked hard to perfect each picture. When I entered an art contest, I was a winner! Then I wanted to be an artist.

When I grew up, I made a career of my two favorite things. I became an artist and a writer. For many years, I worked in New York, publishing stories for children. I worked with an editor. We chose the art and the photos.

The title of the first story I wrote is *Totem Pole*. It tells how David and his father make a totem pole.

To write this story, I went to visit David in the state of Washington. I found out many new things in the time I spent there. I watched as the totem pole was made. David's family and friends told me folktales. They were fine retellers of these old stories.

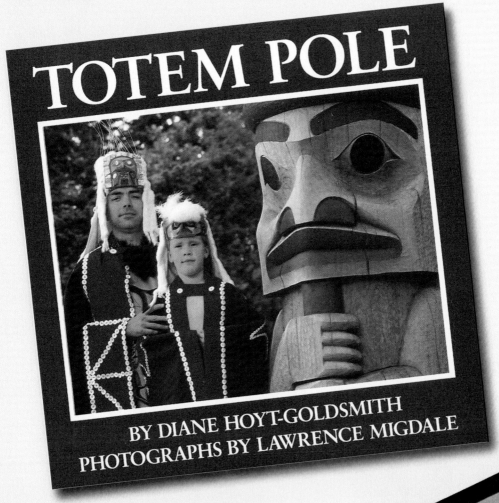

TOTEM POLE

BY DIANE HOYT-GOLDSMITH
PHOTOGRAPHS BY LAWRENCE MIGDALE

For a true story, an author must get all the facts. I used a tape recorder when I spoke with David. I also wrote many notes. My notes and the tape recordings helped me remember what I found out.

My friend Mr. Migdale did the photos of David and the totem pole. I used these pictures so readers could see what I wrote about. I wrote the story so others could see how totem poles are made.

When I wrote the story, I used a computer.
That way I could correct mistakes with ease.
I had to revise my writing many times before
I was finished.

My first published story was a success!
Many children liked to read about David and
the totem pole.

Now I am the author of many true stories.
I make it a rule to tell about real children and
real things.

Each time I start a new story, I go somewhere different. In my career as an author, I have traveled more than 100,000 miles. I have made new friends in many states.

As a girl, I traveled far and wide by reading. Now my stories help children do the same. Now I travel for real and do all the things I used to dream about!

Think About It

1. What did the author have to do to write her first book?

2. Why do you think the author writes true stories?

3. Write a letter to the author of "This Is My Story." Tell her what you liked most about her story.

Fact and Opinion

In "This Is My Story" there are many facts about the author's life. Sometimes writers also give their opinions about things. A **fact** is a statement that can be checked. An **opinion** tells what someone thinks or feels.

Fact or Opinion?

Is It a Fact?	Is It an Opinion?
Can it be checked? Could someone show that it is true?	Does it tell someone's feelings? Does the writer use words that show feelings, such as *good* or *bad*?
Example I worked with an editor.	**Example** They were fine retellers of these old stories.

It is important for readers to be able to tell a fact from an opinion. Readers can then form their own ideas about what they read.

Read these sentences. Which is a fact and which is an opinion?

I became an artist and a writer.

The best stories are about faraway lands or other times.

The Big Snow

by Sharon Fear

illustrated by John Manders

When I started this job, the boss, Moe, showed me around. "Fellows," he said to the ranch hands, "Bob has run off again. You know he always goes before the big snow."

Low grumbling came from the men.

"Whoa, fellows!" said Moe. "Show some manners. Meet Joe. Joe here will fix your meals from now on."

Moe showed me the cupboard. It was supplied with the bare necessities. I couldn't feed the men a varied menu on that. I said so to Moe.

"These fellows don't know a varied menu from a snowdrift," Moe said. "Big portions of anything they can eat. That's a meal to them."

I said I'd do my best.

For the morning meal, I'd make a wagonload of
oatmeal and toast. For lunch, I'd serve chili in bowls as
big as bathtubs. For dinner, I'd roast some beef.

When I was not roasting or toasting, I was baking
cakes. The fellows liked something sweet after dinner.

No one ever said, "Good lunch, Joe," or "Fine dinner,
Joe." But their moans and groans told me they liked it.

My stock began to run low. I started to town for
more . . .

. . . just as the big snow came.

It began uneventfully. Some drizzle. Some rain. It rained until the rain turned to snow. Then it became the snowstorm of all snowstorms. Did it blow! The road to town was closed. I had to turn back.

"It's like this each winter," said Moe.

So that's why Bob always left before the big snow. He was smart!

I was alarmed. If the fellows were expecting a meal and there wasn't one, they would get mean. "Moe!" I said. "How will I feed the men?"

"I don't know, Joe," said Moe.

Well, I wouldn't abandon the men the way Bob did. So I made do with what I had.

All winter the fellows ate my Oak Leaf Salad and my Slow-Roasted Cactus. They said my Lizard Loaf was not bad. My Horned Toad on Toast . . . Well, they ate it.

But the cupboard was about picked clean. All we had lots of was snow. Hmmm . . . What goes with snow? Spaghetti and Snowballs? No. Toasted Oats Floating on Snow? No. Snow-Coated Crows' Toes? No, no, NO!

Then it hit me like a snowslide.

I milked the goat. I mixed goat's milk with snow. I added something sweet. I tasted it. Mmmm! Just like . . . !

I put it into bowls. "Fellows," I said. "Taste my Big Snow."

They dug in. "Mmmm!" they moaned. "Oooo!" they groaned. "Sweet. Just like . . . !"

"That's right!" I said.

Moe, the fellows, and I ate bowls and bowls of
Big Snow that winter. We damaged our waistlines
some. We ate all the snow off the road, too! At last
we could get to town and get something else to eat.

Not that the men were tired of my Lizard Loaf.
Not at all, they said. They just had to have some
cake to go with their Big Snow.

Think About It

1. Why does the ranch give Joe a job? Does he do his job well?

2. Do the ranch hands get fatter or thinner that winter? How do you know?

3. You have a job at Joe's cafeteria. Write a menu that shows what will be served today. Invent some dishes of your own, too!

GOOD ADVICE

a play by Meish Goldish
illustrated by Christiane Beauregard

Who's in the Play

Mrs. Gold	Mr. Gold
Peter	Jo
Brian	Ms. Post
Speaker	

Time: A Friday morning in the middle of summer.

Stage setting: The Gold home; we can see the yard outside as well as the inside of the house.

Mrs. Gold: Peter! Jo! Brian! Please don't leave your things in the middle of the room where I can keep falling over them!

Peter: But Mom, where can we put them?

Jo: There's no room anywhere.

Brian: Our house is so tiny! We're bumping elbows each time we turn around.

Mrs. Gold: I know, but there's no way to fix this problem.

Peter: Father, can you find us a bigger house?

Mr. Gold: No, we can't afford a bigger house. I'll speak with Ms. Post, because she is the wisest person in town. She may have some ideas or some good advice.

159

Speaker: One morning, Ms. Post came over to the Gold home.

Mr. Gold: *(looking sad)* Hi, Ms. Post. Thank you for stopping by. My family has a big problem.

Ms. Post: What kind of problem?

Mr. Gold: Our house is so tiny that we have no room. We have a dreadful time moving about. What can we do?

Ms. Post: I see you have hens in your yard. Bring them into the house with you.

Mr. Gold: But Ms. Post, I'm confused. How will that help?

Ms. Post: Just do as I say and you'll see. Good day. *(She leaves.)*

Speaker: Mr. Gold let the hens into the house.

Peter: Father! What are you doing?

Jo: We can't have hens in our tiny house!

Brian: *(wailing)* I just stepped on an egg and now it's broken!

Mrs. Gold: There are feathers all over! Get those hens out of here!

Mr. Gold: We must follow Ms. Post's advice. She said to bring them in, and we will keep them in until I can speak with her again. After all, she is the wisest person in town.

Mrs. Gold: Please ask her to return. Tell her we have no room!

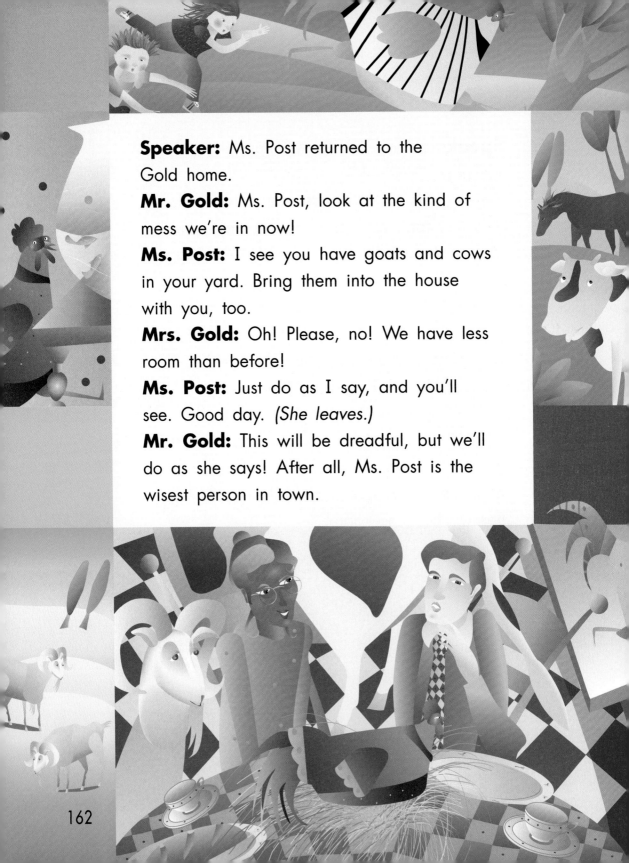

Speaker: Ms. Post returned to the Gold home.

Mr. Gold: Ms. Post, look at the kind of mess we're in now!

Ms. Post: I see you have goats and cows in your yard. Bring them into the house with you, too.

Mrs. Gold: Oh! Please, no! We have less room than before!

Ms. Post: Just do as I say, and you'll see. Good day. *(She leaves.)*

Mr. Gold: This will be dreadful, but we'll do as she says! After all, Ms. Post is the wisest person in town.

Speaker: Mr. Gold let the goats and both cows come in.

Peter: Father, hold on a moment! How can you do this?

Jo: We have no room for goats and cows in here!

Brian: I'm sitting on a goat!

Mr. Gold: We must trust Ms. Post. She told me to bring them in, and we all know that she is the wisest person in town.

Mrs. Gold: Please ask her to return. Tell her we have no room!

Speaker: Ms. Post returned to the Gold home.

Ms. Post: How are you faring now, Mr. Gold?

Mr. Gold: We're going out of our minds! We've lost our wits! We have no room for all these animals!

Ms. Post: *(smiling)* Then take them outside again. Farewell, Mr. Gold. *(She leaves. He takes all the animals back into the yard.)*

Peter: Father! Our house seems so much bigger now!

Mrs. Gold: We have so much more room!

Mr. Gold: I told you! Ms. Post gives good advice.

Think About It

1. What problem did the Golds have? What advice did Ms. Post give them?

2. Do you think Ms. Post gives the Golds good advice? Tell why you think as you do.

3. Think of some good advice a wise person has given you. Write a short story to a younger child that shows why this advice is good to follow.

Auction Day

by Carol Storment

illustrated by Anthony Carnabuci

When Ty spied the pony in the pen of wild horses, he knew what he had to do. First he went to the bank.

"How much money do I have?" he asked.

The man smiled. "You're a rich man, Tyrone. You have six dollars."

"Is that enough for that pony outside?" asked Ty.

The man looked out the window. "Oh no, Ty. Those horses will go for ten dollars or more. Besides, what good would a wild pony be on a farm?"

Ty didn't say another word. He went across the road to the store. Ty had a plan to get his pony.

"Is there any work I could do for you, Mrs. Wyman?" Ty asked. "I need some extra money."

The storekeeper said, "Why yes, Tyrone. I'll find something for you to do."

Ty started by sweeping up. All morning he worked around the store, stacking shelves and cleaning the back room. When he was done, Mrs. Wyman gave him a dollar.

Ty walked by the pen full of wild horses. There she was, the littlest pony. Her coat was so black, it was almost blue. "Hello, Blue Sky," Ty said. He put out his hand. The shy pony jumped away. Her eyes were wild, but they looked sad, too.

"Be brave, girl!" Ty said. "You'll be out of here tomorrow."

The next day, Ty went to see three of his neighbors. He asked each one, "Is there work I can do for you?"

"You bet there is!" they all said.

First, Ty cut tall grass for Mr. Dyer. Then he moved a pile of rocks for Mr. Ryan. He fed chickens and collected eggs for Mrs. Bly. He worked until Mrs. Bly fried some eggs for his lunch. She asked Ty what he needed the money for.

"A pony" was all he would say. Then he went back to work. Ty tried his best to do each task well. He wanted his neighbors to be satisfied with his work.

When Ty was done, each neighbor was happy and paid him one dollar. Now he had three more dollars! The neighbors watched as he left for home. "That Tyrone works hard," they all agreed. "But he'll have his hands full if he tries to tame a wild pony!"

When Ty got home, he got out his bank. He counted all his money. Then he borrowed a horse and rode as fast as he could into town. He ran to the bank. It was still open.

"I'll take my six dollars, please," Ty told the man.

The man smiled. "Here you go. Good luck at the sale tomorrow!"

The sale started early. Everyone in the county came to see the wild horses. Ty was there with his money clutched in his hand.

The auctioneer called out that it was time to start. The bids began. The horses were going for much more than ten dollars. Ty felt like crying. He wouldn't have enough money!

At last only Blue Sky was left. Ty bid ten dollars. Everyone in town knew how much Ty wanted that pony. No one said a word.

"Sold!" shouted the auctioneer. "That pony is all yours, son."

All of Ty's neighbors clapped for him.

Ty and his family got Blue Sky home and into her new pen. Ty sat and watched her for a while. Her blue-black coat was glistening in the sun. Her mane was flying in the wind. But her eyes were still wild and sad. Then Ty got up and opened the gate. Blue Sky shot out and galloped away.

His father ran up. "Ty! Why did you let the pony get away? You worked so hard to get the money for her!"

Ty said, "Blue Sky would never be happy living on a farm. I was glad to spend my money to set her free."

Ty felt proud as his pony galloped to freedom. *Fly away, Blue Sky!*

Think About It

1. What does Ty do so that he can buy Blue Sky?

2. Why do you think Ty doesn't tell anyone he plans to set Blue Sky free?

3. Write the diary entry Ty might write the day he lets Blue Sky go.

Characters' Feelings and Actions

Ty sets Blue Sky free because he feels sorry for the sad-looking pony. The way story characters act can show you how they feel.

To know how a character feels, think about what the character says and does. Look for words the author or other characters use to describe him or her.

This chart shows what Ty does when the auction is about to start. It shows his feelings, too.

Action	Feeling
clutches his money in his hand	worried about the auction

On a sheet of paper, chart a story character's actions and feelings. List some actions from another story you know, and then write the feeling each one shows you.

Action	Feeling

Action	Feeling

The Little Brown Quail

by Cheyenne Cisco

illustrated by Don Sullivan

Brother Quail had a neat little house in the desert, where the wind blew the tumbleweeds. He had dug a swimming hole there, too. All the desert cousins came to his house to lie in the shade. It was good to relax out of the bright sunlight. They sipped tea and ate corn chips. Mmm! Brother Quail made the best corn chips under the sun.

174

"It's time to make the corn chips!" said Brother Quail one bright day. "Now, first things first! Who will help me pick the corn?"

"I will," said Fox, "but wait! I see something suspicious over by that cactus." He escaped across the sand.

"I might," said Little Owl, "but I fly at night. Wake me when there's starlight." He shut his eyes.

"All right," said Brother Quail. "I will pick the corn myself." And he did. The sun burned bright. The hot desert wind blew. But Brother Quail picked every ear.

"Now, who will help me grind the corn?" he asked.

His quail cousins sighed. "We'd like to," they said, "but not right now. We are off to seek our fortunes." They escaped out the window. Flap! Flap! Flap! They were in flight.

"All right," said Brother Quail. "I will grind the corn myself." And he did. He worked all day and all night.

Brother Quail fried the corn chips, too. When he had asked for help, no one would budge. He might as well have been invisible. Brother Quail gave a sigh. He kept right on working.

In a short time, the kitchen was filled with the delightful smell of fresh corn chips. The smell blew out the window. It tickled the noses of Fox and Owl and all the cousins.

They came running.

"Are the chips ready?" asked Fox.

"Stop right there," said Brother Quail. "Why would I give you any? You did not help me pick the corn. You did not help me grind it. You did not help me fry the chips."

"No," said Owl, "but we'd be glad to help you eat them."

"We'll help next time," said Fox.

Brother Quail sighed. Why fight it? They were his friends and cousins after all. "All right," he said.

All the desert cousins thanked Brother Quail for the wonderful chips.

"You're welcome," said Brother Quail. "Now, tell me. Who is going to help clean up the house?"

"Owl will help you," said Fox.

"Let Fox help you," said Owl.

"Oh, no!" sighed Brother Quail.

Then Fox and Owl laughed.

"We are just kidding," they said.

"We will *all* help you." And they did.

Think About It

1. List three jobs Brother Quail does without help. When do the other animals say they will help him?

2. What suspicious thing do you think Fox sees by the cactus? Why do you think that?

3. Think of a fable or folktale you know well. How would the characters be different if the story took place somewhere else? Choose a new setting for the story, and rewrite it in your words.

HARVEST TIME

by Sydnie Meltzer Kleinhenz
illustrated by Cheryl Kirk Noll

"It's harvest time, Lizzie," Dad said.

Mom said, "How about a harvest party tomorrow?"

I clapped my hands. Dad nodded. "Everybody bring a memory-maker," he called as he hurried off to work.

We don't always get a harvest from our banana trees. Bananas grow well in the tropics, but we live on Galveston Island. Sometimes the Texas winter is too cold for banana plants. Sometimes a tropical storm blows off the flowers. Then no fruit can grow. The years we do get bananas, we have a harvest party.

On Saturday morning I went to the trading market. I was looking for a memory-maker. At last I found the perfect thing—a tiny plastic sailing schooner. It was a bargain, so I got it and ran home.

First, I glued the little ship on the inside of a jar lid. Next, I put glitter and water in the jar. Last, I put on the lid and taped around it. I finished the memory-maker just as Dad called, "Harvest time, party time!"

We all met on a blanket on the grass. When I looked up, it seemed as if the banana leaves reached as high as the sky. Some of the bananas were still green. Some were as yellow as the bus I ride each day.

Dad put my spelling folder on the blanket. "Here is my memory-maker," he said. "I'm thankful to my Grandma and Grandpa Jakoby. When they came to America, they studied hard to speak English. That helped them find good jobs and get this fine house."

Mom's memory-maker was a mixing bowl. "I'm thankful that Grandma and Grandpa Jakoby planted bananas. Now we can eat them as snacks or bake tasty treats with them."

I turned my memory-maker upside down and gave it a shake. The glitter looked like swirly snow around the ship.

"I'm thankful that Dad's Grandma and Grandpa Jakoby left their cold and snowy home. I'm glad the ship sailed safely to Galveston Island. I like living where it's mostly warm and sunny."

Mom gave me a squeeze. "You're not the only one who likes it sunny," she said.

Dad told the rest of our family story. Then he got his machete and said, "Let's cut bananas."

Mom and I helped support the bunch as Dad cut the stem. It felt as if we were holding a big log up in the air! My arms were rubbery when we softly set the bananas on the blanket.

We packed small bunches of bananas in bags and carried them to our neighbors. Then it was party time!

First we broke bananas into the blender. Mom added milk, Dad added sweetener, and I added ice. Dad hit the button to whir the mix into milkshakes. The river of banana foam felt frosty all the way down to my belly! We put the extra drink mix into molds to freeze solid. We would have banana ice pops for later.

After that, we mashed bananas to a pulp. We made pans and pans of banana muffins. Some were to give away. Some were to freeze and save. We nibbled banana muffins as we cleaned up.

I filled up on plenty of banana treats. And we all made plenty of memories to last until next harvest time.

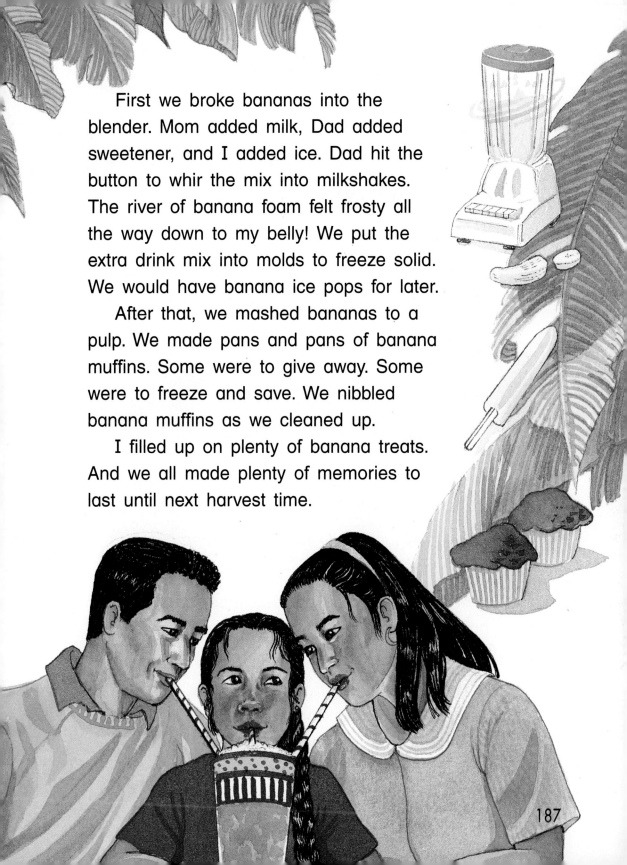

Think About It

1. Why does the family bring memory-makers to the harvest party?

2. How often do Lizzie and her mom and dad have a harvest party? How do you know?

3. The next time they get bananas, Lizzie invites other family members to the harvest party. Make the invitation she sends. Use words and pictures in the invitation.

Summarize

Lizzie's dad tells the family story at the harvest party. To **summarize** the story, Lizzie would tell just the most important things that happen.

A story summary is much shorter than the story. The events are told in order and in your own words.

Read the sentences in the box. They give a summary of "Harvest Time."

> It was time to have a harvest party.
> Lizzie, her dad, and her mom shared their memory-makers.
> Then they harvested the bananas and took some to their neighbors.
> The family made banana treats.

Now read these sentences. Tell why each sentence doesn't belong in a summary of "Harvest Time."

Some Texas winters are too cold for banana plants.
Lizzie found the plastic schooner at the market.

Think about a story you know. What are the most important things that happen? Write a summary of the story.

A Cookie for the Cowboys

by Caren B. Stelson
illustrated by Jerry Tiritilli

Howdy, partner! Glad to have you riding along on this cattle drive. My name's George Gemson, but you can call me Cookie. Everyone does. My job is to cook for all you cowhands out on the range. You stay on the good side of me and you won't go hungry.

You look like a greenhorn to me. You know what
that means? You're a brand-new hand. I'm sure the
trail boss is a fair judge of skill, so you must be good
with horses. I've been on more than my share of cattle
drives. I'll tell you what's in store for you.

Tending cattle is hard work. You'll be riding a horse all day long. You'll be very dirty. You'll eat dust. We'll move the cattle north slowly, so they have time to eat and grow fat. Keep an eye out for stray cows. These ranchers want their cattle herds to bring a good price in the market. They want to make money—a profit. That's OK by me. Then we'll all be paid.

The day starts early on a cattle drive. You'll be up at sunrise. I'll be up before that. I start breakfast at three in the morning. First, I make up a roaring campfire. Next, I bake the rolls. Then I make the coffee. Last, I put the beans in the pot and fry up the bacon. All this takes time. I won't nudge you gently to wake you up. When I holler that breakfast is ready, you'd better come running.

This is my wagon. It's called a chuck wagon. Mr. Charles Goodnight made the first one in 1866. He got an old army wagon and nailed a dresser to the back of it. Folks called Mr. Goodnight "Chuck." Maybe that's how this wagon got its name. Greenhorn, this wagon will be your home away from home.

I'll show you what I mean. I keep everything in
this dresser. I keep all the dry stuff in this one.
Here's the flour, beans, coffee—and the honey, too.
Here is where I keep the tin plates, cups, and forks.
This one is for the trail boss. He keeps his papers
and maps safe in my chuck wagon.

This next one holds stuff for any doctoring I might have to do on the trail. If a snake bites you, let me know. If you want a haircut, you let me know about that, too. I'm a jack-of-all-trades.

Well, partner, I can't talk all day. You go on over to the corral. Pick out a gentle horse that's been well tamed. Then be ready for the time of your life. Yippee!

Think About It

1. Is Cookie's job easy? What kinds of things does he do?

2. Why does Cookie start cooking breakfast at three in the morning?

3. Cookie is important to the cowboys. Write a poem or words to a song that the cowboys might write about their cook.

PENNY SAVERS

written by Meish Goldish
illustrated by Mary Jones

"A penny saved is a penny earned."

Did you ever hear that saying? It means that if you can hold on to money and not spend it, you have really earned it.

Why save your money? What's the point?
Why not spend it right away and enjoy it now?

The Boyd family knows why. Let's see what they have found out.

Roy Boyd will turn nine years old on his birthday this month. Each year, Roy receives money for his birthday. He likes to spend it right away. He spends each dollar and doesn't save a thing.

Last year, Roy went to the toy store the day after his birthday. He got a yo-yo and a ball. The next week he found a toy car he wanted. He couldn't buy it because he had no more money.

This year, Roy will save his birthday money until he knows all his choices. Then he'll buy what he wants most.

Roy has found out why it's smart to save.

Joy Boyd is Roy's sister. Like Roy, Joy gets money each year for her birthday. Like Roy, she likes to spend each dollar right away.

This year Joy wants to get skates, but she did not receive enough money to buy them.

At first, Joy said to herself, "The skates cost too much. I guess I'll have to buy something that costs less."

Then Joy had an idea. "I'll save all my birthday money this year," she said. "Maybe I can work to earn the rest of the money I'll need to buy the skates."

Joy has discovered how it helps to save.

Mrs. Boyd knows that a penny saved is a penny earned. In fact, she saves more than just pennies. She saves all kinds of coins.

Sometimes Mrs. Boyd rides the bus to work. The driver does not take dollar bills, so the riders must pay with combinations of coins. If they don't have coins, they can't ride.

All week, Mrs. Boyd makes it a point to save her coins. She uses dollar bills to pay for things and saves her change. That way, she'll have coins when she wants to ride the bus.

Like his wife, Mr. Boyd spends his money carefully. He knows the value of a dollar and that it pays to save.

Mr. Boyd puts the money he earns in a bank. Why? First of all, he knows the money is safe there and that it won't get lost. Mr. Boyd and his wife go to the bank and take out cash when they need it. They can also pay for things by writing checks. Then the bank sends the money to the person who received the check.

When the Boyds save money in a bank, they make money, too! That's because the bank pays them to save their money there. If you save your money in a bank, you'll make money, too!

It really does "pay" to save!

The Boyds have found out something else about saving money. You never know when you'll need it!

Last year, it rained very hard on the Boyds' home. The roof began to leak and needed to be fixed right away.

The Boyds hired someone to fix their roof. It cost a lot of money. What if they had not saved? They could not have had the work done, and the rain would have left their home soiled and spoiled.

You never know when you may need money. That's why it's wise to "save for a rainy day."

Now you know why the Boyds save their money. They know that it is important to make choices about spending and saving. You may wish to save, too. How can you get started?

You may receive some money as a gift on your birthday. Maybe you can earn an allowance for doing chores around the house. You might make the beds, sweep the floor, and take out the trash. You could also offer to clean the yard for your neighbors.

You may think of a hundred ways to make money! A hundred jobs may get you a hundred dollars or more. If you can save it, congratulations!

Think About It

1. What reasons does the author give for saving money?

2. What does "saving for a rainy day" mean?

3. The Boyd family is having a meeting. They are talking about what to do with $50 that Grandma sent them. Write what each person might say.

BOOK OF DAYS

written by
Deborah Akers

illustrated by
Mercedes McDonald

Date: April 2

Dear Sue,

I felt so blue after you drove away! Now I have a plan. I will keep each day in this book until my big sister is home again. Then you can read about everything you missed, and I will feel less lonely.

I put myself in charge of your flower box. There were three new green sprouts in the soil. You said there would soon be a rainbow of flowers. I poured a little more water to hurry them along. I could tell they wondered where you were.

Date: April 6

Dear Sue,

Today was a good day. We worked in the garden, and Mom put me in charge of the carrot seeds. I pushed them into the dirt the way you showed me.

Remember last fall, when we dug beds for the plants to sleep in? Most of them are still sleeping, but a few seem to be stirring. The sweet pea sprouts are reaching for the sun with soft, curly fingers.

Date: April 9

Dear Sue,

Today I put myself in charge of the fruit trees. I walked down every row, and counted all the trees that have buds.

Here is a branch from the apple tree. Remember when we picked a basketful of apples? Then you helped me bake my first pie. I felt like a real cook!

The trees seem as if they are holding secrets in their tight buds. I think they are waiting for the right person to share them with. I know just how they feel.

Date: April 13

Dear Sue,

   Today was an average day. While Mom went into town, Dad and I walked down to the river. I collected rocks for you on the beach. There were lots of beautiful ones, but I was choosy. I took just a few you could put on your desk.

   Guess what happened next? I saw tracks in the sand! Our friend the fox is back, with some baby foxes, too. That must mean spring is really here. When will you be home? You're missing everything!

Date: April 21

Dear Sue,

Today the sky could not stop crying, and your flower box was swimming in rain. I watched from the porch as pools grew in the garden. The fruit trees shook in the storm.

A good thing happened today, too—there was a rainbow. I remembered the special rainbow wish we always make when it rains. I made my wish. Mom said she had a feeling it would come true soon.

Date: April 22

Dear Sue,

Mom was right! I woke up to a sunny day and ran outside. I think the garden must have heard a signal in the night. There were leaves and blooms and little celebrations everywhere!

Then came the best news! You are coming home tonight! Now I am putting myself in charge of the biggest celebration of all!

Think About It

1. Why does the girl write in her book of days? What does she write about?

2. Do you think the girl in the story will go on writing in her book of days? Tell why you think as you do.

3. Imagine that a friend or family member is out of town. Write a journal entry for a special day you would want him or her to know about.

Important Details

The main character in "Book of Days" writes letters to help her feel less lonely while her sister is away. The author gives details that tell you more about this main idea. **Details** answer questions like these:

Who?   *What?*   *Where?*

When?   *How?*   *Why?*

Here is a web that shows a main idea and some details.

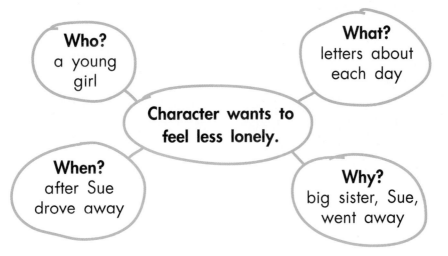

Who?
a young girl

What?
letters about each day

Character wants to feel less lonely.

When?
after Sue drove away

Why?
big sister, Sue, went away

Each of the girl's letters to her sister has a main idea and some details. Choose one letter, and make a web like the one shown. Show at least three details that give more information about the main idea.

THE HUMMINGBIRD

·GARDEN·

Cyrus already knew what Dad would say. He had to ask anyway.

"Dad, may we get a pet? Please! We really need a pet around here."

"You know we can't have a pet," Dad said. "The rule is no dogs in this building. Hamsters make you sneeze, and the city is no place for a pony!"

WRITTEN BY JOSÉ GONZALES
ILLUSTRATED BY JOUNG UN KIM

Cy smiled at Dad's little joke, but he still felt bad.

Then Dad said, "I have an idea. City birds need help. You can use the backyard to make a garden for them. The birds can be your pets."

"Oh, Dad," Cy said. "Our backyard is made of cement! There's no space for a garden out there!" He knew Dad was doing his best, but he didn't understand how that idea could work.

"You can make space," Dad said. "You can use things our neighbors throw out to plant flowers in. You can dig up dirt to put in them. I'll give you a few dollars to get seeds and a bird feeder."

"I'll try it," said Cy. Maybe Dad's idea was not so bad after all.

That same evening, Cy looked through bird books.

"I want our bird visitors to be hummingbirds," Cy told Dad.

"Good idea," Dad replied. "Our little garden has ample space for such tiny birds."

"Hummingbirds catch and eat bugs," Cy went on. "They drink the nectar from flowers. Sometimes they drink sweet water from a feeder, too. They like red and pink flowers best, so I'll plant red and pink flowers to attract them to the garden. Once they're here, they'll find the feeder. Then they'll know where to visit when they're thirsty."

Cy looked through the neighbors' junk. He picked up old boxes and pails, then he poked holes in the bottoms so the water would drain out. When Mrs. Cecil found out what he was doing, she gave him old pots from her cellar. Cy filled everything with dirt.

Soon Cy was ready to get his seeds. Dad gave him some money and took him to the shopping center.

Back at home, Cy dug little furrows in the dirt and planted seeds for red flowers. He watered the seeds each day and watched for signs of growth.

When Cy spied red flowers in his garden, he mixed up some sweet water. He filled the hummingbird feeder. Then he waited for thirsty hummingbirds.

Cy watched from morning to evening. No little visitors showed up. It seemed that the hummingbirds had shunned his beautiful garden.

Then one summer day Cy spotted a tiny blur. Could it be? Yes! It was a hummingbird. It raced around the garden like a small cyclone. Its wings were going like little windmills. It found the feeder, and soon more hummingbirds joined it.

Each day, Cy's visitors returned. They circled the flowers and sucked sweet water from the feeder. Cy could see their red throats. He looked in his bird book and found that they were ruby-throated hummingbirds.

In the evenings, Cy took down the feeder. He cleaned it out and filled it with fresh sweet water. Then he put it up again. He knew the daytime heat would bring his visitors back.

Cy liked to watch the tiny birds. Their wings went so fast that they were just a blur. They could hang in one place like a helicopter! Cy cherished the time he spent with his new pets.

The days got shorter, and there was less heat. Summer turned to fall. One day the hummingbirds did not return. Cy missed his little pets, but he knew they had to go south. They could not stand winter's snow and ice.

He cleaned the feeder one last time and put it away. He knew he would need it again. Next spring he would plant a new garden. He would put up the feeder, and his pets would visit again. Cy had turned his cement backyard into a very nice place for hummingbirds.

Think About It

1. What does Cy do to make a garden for his pets? How long do his pets stay?

2. How do you think Cy's dad feels about the changes Cy makes in the garden? Tell why you think as you do.

3. A newspaper reporter came and looked at Cy's hummingbird garden. She took pictures and wrote a news story about what Cy had done. Write the newspaper story, and draw a picture to go with it.

A MOUNTAIN
BLOWS ITS TOP

A chain of mountains runs along the west coast of North America. It's called the Cascade Range.

The mountains in this range are beautiful. Visitors hike and camp there. Loggers cut trees for lumber. Birds and animals make their homes in the forests, fields, and rivers.

STORY BY KANA RILEY

These peaks were formed long ago by volcanoes. Deep in the center of our planet is hot melted rock called magma. On top of it float plates of hard rock that form the planet's crust.

In 1980 the plates under the Cascade Range started to shift. The edges of the plates pushed up magma. As the magma rose, it caused the north side of Mount St. Helens to bulge. It made the ground shake. Plumes of steam began to shoot out of the old crater, or hole, at the top. Was the mountain ready to blow? No one knew.

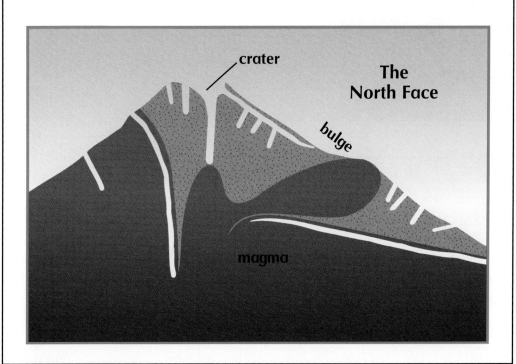

Sunday, May 18, 1980, dawned clear. Snowcapped Mount St. Helens caught the early rays of the sun. All seemed peaceful.

Then suddenly, at 8:32 A.M., the ground began to shake. The epicenter of this quake was very near Mount St. Helens.

This was a big one! With a mighty blast, it cracked the side of the mountain. Magma gushed to the surface, pushing layers of dirt and rocks and water in front of it. Blast after blast rocked the mountain.

Blocks of ice went flying. Water turned to steam. Rocks exploded into dust. Hot ash flew 12 miles into the sky.

Yakima, Washington, is 85 miles from Mount St. Helens. By 9:30 A.M. the sky in Yakima began to grow black. Lightning flashed. It looked as if a storm were coming.

But it was not rain that fell. It was ash. The tiny bits had edges as sharp as glass. They hurt everyone's eyes and made it hard to breathe.

All day ash fell. Soon every surface was covered with layers of it. Workers later swept up more than 600,000 tons from the streets and buildings.

When the big blasts stopped, Mount St. Helens was an awesome sight. The top of the mountain was not there. In its place was a huge, gray hole. From the center of it, clouds of ash still puffed into the air.

The land around the mountain looked like the surface of the moon. All was still. Trees were spilled all over the ground like match sticks. Rivers were choked with mud. Most of the animals had been caught by the blasts. No birds sang.

It has been many years since the mountain blew. What has Mount St. Helens taught us?

It has taught us that our planet is always changing. The blast showed us the awesome damage these changes can cause.

Yet we also saw that in time the land will heal. New plants now grow out of the layers of ash. Animals have come back. The rivers run clear once more.

What's going on inside the mountain? It's not quiet yet. In the center of the crater, another dome of magma is growing. Sometimes steam and ash gush out of it. They help us remember that our planet is still alive and still shaking.

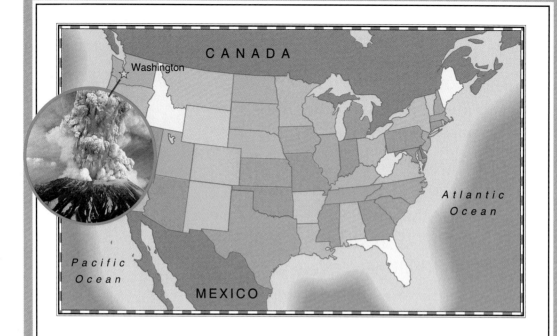

Think About It

1. What happened when Mount St. Helens erupted? What has happened since then?

2. Will Mount St. Helens erupt again? What makes you think as you do?

3. Think about life in Yakima on the day Mount St. Helens blew its top. Write a diary entry as if you were there that day.

Cause and Effect

Mount St. Helens erupted in 1980. "A Mountain Blows Its Top" tells some of the reasons it erupted.

When you read, think about why things happen. Why something happens is the **cause**. What happens is the **effect**.

This chart shows a cause and an effect from "A Mountain Blows Its Top."

Cause	Effect
The plates under the Cascade Range shifted.	The magma rose.

To find a cause, ask *"Why did this happen?"* To find an effect, ask *"What happened?"*

Look at this picture. Think about what is happening. Think about why it is happening. Write one sentence that tells the cause. Write another sentence that tells the effect.

THE PLACE IN SPACE

Written by Susan M. Fischer
Illustrated by Paul Meisel

Mom came into my room and sat on the edge of my bed. "Good night, Will," she said, wrapping her cool hand around my wrist. "Where are you off to tonight?" she asked. "Grandma's garden? The lake? The moon?" Mom knew that my dreams could take me places.

"I just might go far out into the universe, Mom," I said. "I bet I could explore the entire world in a single night!"

She smiled and said, "I bet you could, too, dear. Sweet dreams." She pulled the blanket she knitted for me right up to my chin. "You can tell me all about it in the morning," she said with a wink.

"Sure, Mom." I yawned as she turned on my night-light. It's a blue-and-green sphere that glows as it twirls. I watched it for a while. Eventually I fell asleep.

At first I wondered where I was, but then I knew.
I was on top of my very own mountain. I'd been
here a thousand times before, but it had never looked
as beautiful as this. I could see the entire city where
I live. I found the winding river and the town hall.

Up above me, a bird was circling—my friend the
wren. She was calling to me. "Yes! Here I come!" I
replied. I soared up and followed her. Up and away
we flew, higher and higher!

As we sailed over misty, puffy clouds, I looked
down and saw my entire state, its shape outlined by
a river. It looked just like the map in my classroom.
It got littler and littler as we flew higher and higher.

Soon I could see our country between two big
seas. Our country is as wide as the whole continent!
Up and up and up we flew, as if we were never
going to stop.

ZZZZ

zZZZ

Then I couldn't believe my
eyes. I had to blink several
times. Could it be the world?
I saw our beautiful planet as
a huge, green-and-blue sphere.
There were clouds and light
and darkness all around it. It
was even prettier than my
night-light.

The wren and I watched the
world turn, happy to be together
and to share this sight. Then
the sun began to peek around.
I knew it was almost morning,
and eventually we would have
to begin our long flight
homeward.

There was a little knock at my door.
Mom said, "It's time to rise and shine.
How was your night?"

"Oh, Mom, it was wonderful," I said.
"I wish you could have been there."

My night-light was still glowing as
it twirled. Just then we could hear a bird
singing. I smiled because I knew it was
my friend the wren.

Think About It

1. Where does Will go in his dream? Who goes with him?

2. How do you think Will's mom knows that he travels in his dreams?

3. What would you see if you looked down on your town from up in the sky? Draw a picture showing how things would look. Label the parts of your picture.

A METEOR Stopped Here

by Kana Riley
illustration by Mel Grant

Our planet gets many kinds of visitors from space. Comets are one kind.

A comet is a ball of frozen gases. The gases are the nucleus, or center, of the comet.

Around the nucleus is a cloud. The cloud looks like a tail. That's because a force from the sun called solar wind blows the cloud out behind the comet.

At night a comet glows like a fluorescent light. It reflects light from the sun, and we see that reflected glow.

Comets loop around the sun in orbits. We know some of their orbits well enough to tell when they will pass near us.

Billions of meteors are also part of our solar system. They orbit the sun, too.

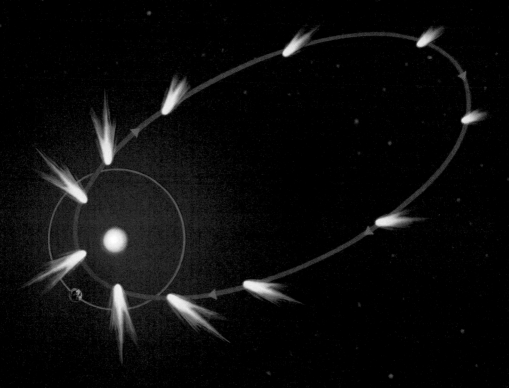

Meteors are different from comets. They are solid, like rock, and most of them show up without warning

Every day, millions of little meteors enter our atmosphere, the air around our planet. Most are tiny particles. They are about the size of a grain of sand.

When these little meteors hit the air, they get hot enough to glow. We see the larger ones as "falling stars" or "shooting stars." Most meteors burn up before they hit the ground.

Once in a very long while, a big meteor comes along. That's what happened 50,000 years ago.

A huge ball of rock 150 feet across came out of the sky. It was speeding toward our planet at 40,000 miles an hour!

The meteor slammed into the ground with the force of 20 million tons of explosives. It made a huge crater 700 feet deep and 4,000 feet across. It tossed rocks the size of elephants as if they were children's blocks.

The meteor itself was destroyed. Part of it was turned into gas, and much of the rest melted. What was left was broken into tiny particles.

That meteor's "autograph" can still be seen in Arizona. The crater is so big that it could hold 20 football games at once.

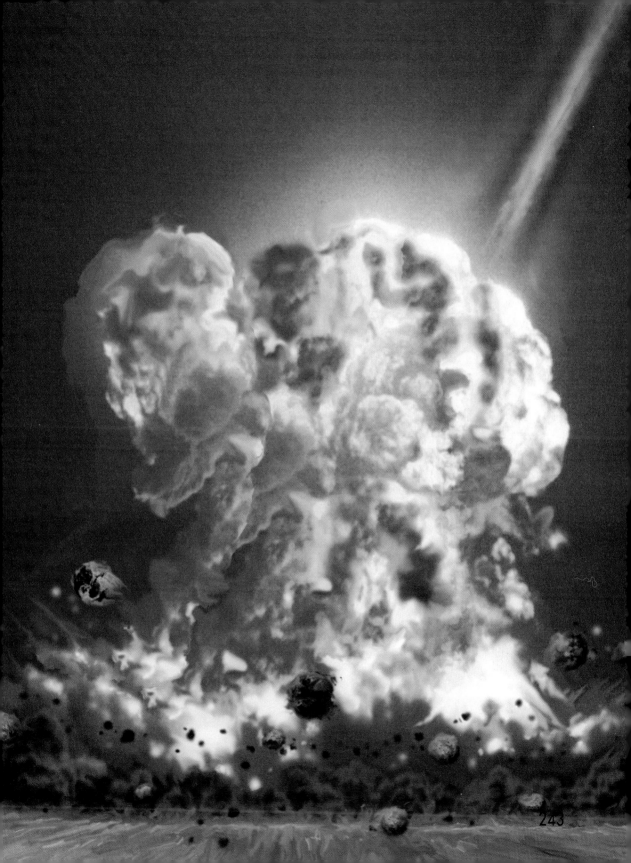

If you go to this meteor crater, you can see the deep trough. Rough, rocky ground lies all around it. You can walk on this rim, but it is tough to do. The ground is still piled high with rocks tossed up by the meteor.

As you take your photographs, you may pause and wonder. When will the next large meteor visit us from space? By then, with enough warning, we may be able to send it back!

Think About It

1. What are meteors? When can we see them?

2. How are comets different from meteors?

3. Make a postcard you could send from the meteor crater in Arizona. Draw a picture for one side of the postcard. For the other side, write a message to a friend.